How to Kayak

The Basics of Kayaking

By

Valerie Howell

How to Kayak: The Basics of Kayaking

Copyright © 2017

All rights reserved. This book or any portion thereof may not be reproduced or used in any manner whatsoever without the express written permission of the publisher except for the use of brief quotations in a book review.

ISBN: 9781522098119

Warning and Disclaimer

Every effort has been made to make this book as accurate as possible. However, no warranty or fitness is implied. The information provided is on an "as-is" basis. The author and the publisher shall have no liability or responsibility to any person or entity with respect to any loss or damages that arise from the information in this book.

Publisher Contact

Skinny Bottle Publishing

books@skinnybottle.com

SKINNY BOTTLE

Introduction	1
Kayaking	5
Getting Started	9
Equipment	13
Safety	26
How to Kayak	37
Ocean and White Water	45
Destination Kayaking and Multi-Day Adventures	49
Conclusion	53

Introduction

You sit in your kayak on a slow-moving river, the boat tracking straight through the water as you effortlessly move your paddle in a slow, relaxing rhythm. In the tall marsh grass, you spot an egret hunting for fish as he watches you pass by, your kayak gliding silently through the water. A fish jumps in the water to your right, a pair of mallards floating ahead of you. You breathe in the fresh air, the feeling of serenity and tranquility that you are experiencing is a result of being in a small boat away from the din of humanity.

To some kayakers, communing with nature, spending time in the quiet places far away from the stress of their ordinary lives is the reason why they enjoy this past time. Yet, this does not explain all that kayaking is and the variety of experiences this sport offers. To every kayaker, there is a certain aspect, a type of kayaking that appeals to each paddler.

As a beginner, you may be wondering, what is the appeal of kayaking and how can it be different for each paddler? Is it the feel of the water under a small boat, the paddle in your hands, the course entirely determined by your sense of adventure?

Could it be the thrill of the white water, your kayak moving quickly, nimbly through the rapids? Or maybe it is the smell of salt water, the sound of the waves as you glide past the surf breaks? All of these experiences are kayaking, each one expresses the appeal of this dynamic sport.

If you have selected this book, you have discovered the appeal of kayaking, you are about to embark on a journey from observer to participant. Maybe you watched with delight as kayakers paddled along a river or experienced it for yourself on a rented kayak on your beach vacation? The dramatic competitions of kayakers who specialize in braving rapids may have caught your attention on a trip to the mountains. It doesn't matter how you discovered the pleasure of kayaking, you have made the decision to become a kayaker and this book will help you get started.

In this book, you will discover a brief history and an understanding of the sport. Understanding the roots of kayaking will give you an appreciation that it is more than just a modern leisure activity. As you grow as a kayaker, you will be continuing a tradition of paddling that has its roots in ancient history. From its beginnings as a mode of transportation and hunting in the ocean, you will learn how the methods of kayaking were born and how they apply to you, the beginner kayaker.

Kayaking is an easy sport to learn and to enjoy. It is suitable for a wide range of ages and abilities. It can be enjoyed as a family, in a group or in solitude. From the gentle hours spent fishing on the lake to an adventurous multi-day trip, you will discover techniques that will allow you to meet challenges and remain confident in your ability to handle them. You will learn how to stay healthy and safe, and what you can do to enjoy your time in a kayak.

Before you purchase your first kayak, you will need the right information to help you get started. With advice and suggestions that you will find in this book, you will be armed with the knowledge you need to decide what type of boat to purchase and the list of safety equipment that is essential. You will feel confident when you are ready to invest in paddles, life vests and a rack for your vehicle. If you have a body of water and a will to get there, with a few tips and the right knowledge you can become a kayaker.

From the relaxing time spent paddling on a calm lake to the physical demands of kayaking a rushing mountain river, the techniques you will need to master and important tips to transition from one type of paddling to another can be found in this book. You will learn how to paddle and how to steer. Learn how to glide over waves and how to keep your boat and you upright in the water. Once you have learned the basic strokes, you can build on them, learning other techniques from strokes common to fresh water rivers to the ocean and white water.

Whether you choose white water or salt water, or the quiet solitude of a creek, you will want a place you can practice and try out your new-found skills. Traveling with your boat is a true pleasure, the freedom to paddle limited only by your imagination and your skill level. Traveling with your kayak is easy and you find out how to travel with your small boat to your destination, how to plan a day trip or a longer vacation.

When you become a kayaker, you will experience the world through a different lens, you will see possibilities for kayaking that you may never have noticed before your first paddle.

In this book, the pleasures of kayaking will be shared and the techniques and knowledge you need to get the most out of your kayaking experience will be described in easy to understand language and terms. Kayaking is relaxing, fun, thrilling, an adventure and a few hours of leisurely summer activity, it is all these things and more. With a little patience, practice and your own kayak, you can discover the appeal of kayaking for yourself. On the water in your own boat, you will become a kayaker, a journey that begins in the chapters of this book.

Kayaking

In our modern era, kayaking appears at first glance to be a modern sport. Kayaks are designed to suit any water conditions, they sit low in the water and are easily transported, often weighing less than a hundred pounds. The boats can be brightly colored and often manufactured with modern materials. There is a range of activities that you can do with a kayak from fishing to water trails and they fit on top or behind most vehicles. The diminutive boats are ideal personal water craft, suited for nearly every skill and physical level. From sporting goods stores to surf shops, kayaks can be found to suit a wide range of needs and past times.

The versatility of kayaking and the affordability of the sport seem to point to an origin in modern times, but kayaking is far from a technological achievement of the modern era, its roots stretch back into ancient times. The history of kayaking began long before Europeans landed on the shores of the New World. Kayaking was developed by the indigenous peoples of what is now Alaska and Canada. As the empires rose and fell in the Mediterranean, the Aleut people, related to the later Inuit, were developing a method of transporting themselves through the coastal waters. These early boats were made of materials that were available in their environments such as whale skin and bones, and the water-resistant skin of seals.

The native people of the cold North would use these light maneuverable boats to hunt for food and to fish. Kayaks, as the boats were called, were also used to transport themselves and their families across the bodies of the water known as the Bering Sea, the Northwest Passage and the Northern Atlantic. The boats they used were the earliest known kayaks. With their sleek design, these boats with their long narrow bows and sterns would track straight and say stable in choppy and dangerous waves. These boats were so reliable that there are reports made during the Middle Ages of strange people dressed in animal skins reaching the isles of Scotland in this sea going vessels.

In modern times, kayaks are often used by fishermen who prefer the near silent method of paddling for the same reason that the Inuit preferred to use kayaks, these boats glide quietly in the water. They do not startle marine animals or fish like other methods of fishing, an ideal circumstance for the ancient Aleut and the modern sportsman. Fishing from a kayak requires less expense and no fuel to operate, making it an economical alternative to an expensive powered fishing boat.

As a method of transportation across waves and fast-moving bodies of water, kayaking is far more stable than the canoe and the small sail boat. Unlike other styles of small water craft, the low sitting kayak remains stable and depending on the design will be less likely to capsize in rough conditions. The waters of the Northern latitudes are among the roughest and most dangerous in the world. The kayak was designed by the indigenous people to carry them into these unforgiving waters and back home again.

It was the brilliance of the design and the utility of these swift, agile boats that first captured the imagination of Europeans. As the Victorians discovered the far-reaching corners of the world, exploration was fashionable, with every country wanting the honor of discovering a part of the world never seen by Europeans. It was during this era, that the Indigenous people of the North were studied, their way of life documented. Their sea going boats became a source of fascination for many people on the continent as kayaking officially made the jump from North America to Europe in the mid-nineteenth century.

The first Europeans to grasp the concept of kayaking mainly used them to traverse rivers and lakes, this quickly spread to include multi-day adventures. By the early twentieth century, kayaking was capturing the imagination of an emerging middle class in Europe and back to its home in the New World. By the 1930s, kayaking was springing up as a fun and affordable method of transportation for journeys along the coast and down rivers. In the 1950s, kayaking was touted as a family activity and a part of summer fun at camps and lakes. As the century came to an end, kayaking had evolved into what you see today, a versatile sport that appeals to the weekend paddler and the thrill-seeking adrenaline junkie. It is both an Olympic sport and a vacation past time. From eco-tourism to paddling tours, kayaking is changing and adapting as we approach the next decade of the twenty-first century.

As kayaking made its journey from the ocean-going design of the Inuit people to the highly versatile designs of the modern era, it has changed and adapted to the needs of the kayaker. Seal skin and whale bone are no longer the only materials available. The array of kayaks and the material of manufacture are astounding from the inflatable models to the sleek wooden boats, from the short snub nosed white water craft to the long narrow oceanic vessels.

From wood to carbon fiber, kayaking remains true to its ancient roots. Kayaks are still stable, stealthy, reliable and ideal for shallow inlets and deep waters. The paddling techniques of the Inuit braving the waves are no different than the modern thrill seeker diving off cliffs into white water to prove his mettle. The ancient fisherman glided silently across the water to catch fish as do the modern fisherman in rivers across the world.

Kayaking is modern in design and material. The technology may have changed but kayaking remains the same, a graceful method of transporting yourself across the waves in a boat powered entirely by paddle and your own ability. When you are kayaking, you are continuing this long and storied tradition and you are becoming part of that lineage.

Getting Started

Kayaking is not complicated, it is you, sitting in your boat with your paddle in your hands. You are in control of the vessel. You decide which body of water to explore and control all your needs while you are spending time pursuing this relaxing and fun past time. Unlike many other sports that require months of intensive training and expensive equipment, kayaking is affordable and getting started is easy.

As stated previously, kayaking is a past time that is accessible to nearly everyone regardless of age or physical ability. You don't have to be a lifelong athlete to begin kayaking. You can be a ten-year-old child or an eighty-year-old retiree, there is a type of kayaking for you. The physical demands of kayaking are not excessive unless you choose the physically demanding white water or long-distance ocean kayaking.

To begin your kayaking adventure, you will want to begin with one simple question, can you swim? If you are a parent of an older child, can your child swim? You do not have to be an Olympic swimmer or the greatest swimmer but this is a skill that is essential to kayaking. This may seem counterproductive, you are going to be on or in a boat paddling across the water wearing a personal floatation device, why on earth would you need to swim? The answer is simple, it may save your life. Drownings happen in water of all depths, therefore the ability to swim is essential.

Before you decide that kayaking is not for you because you or your child can not swim a mile, don't be discouraged. You only need to be a competent swimmer and know how to tread water, you don't have to master the breast stroke in the 400 meters. It is essential that you know how to keep your head above water and can confidently swim a short distance if it becomes necessary. Once you have established that you feel comfortable in the water without a boat, you are ready to kayak.

The ability to swim is important but there is more to kayaking than preparing for the worst-case scenario. The next physical ability that is essential to kayaking is being able to hold the paddle and move your upper body in a broad range of motion. Although you rely on your hips and lower body to hold you steady in the boat and your core to support your back and your upper body. The real power of the kayak is you and your ability to paddle.

You don't have to be able to power paddle, but you will want to be able to grip the paddle with confidence and move it as necessary to steer and power the boat. In some cases, such as the infamous roll technique, your ability to move the paddle will help you return to an upright position. Your upper body strength may also come in handy if you must portage with your boat or must climb into the boat from the water.   As with swimming, you do not have to be a power lifter or have a high level of upper body strength, but a good range of motion through the shoulders and back is preferable.

Before you begin, you will also want to consider the strength you will need to carry your kayak from your vehicle to the water. This will greatly depend on the type of kayak you select. Many kayaks weigh approximately fifty pounds, these can easily be transported by yourself or with some help from your vehicle to the water and back again. If you need a boat that weighs even less, there are inflatable kayaks and folding boats that are preferred for their ease of transport and their light weight.

Finally, before you consider what equipment to purchase, where will you be kayaking? Although you may be tempted to jump right into class five rapids or crash past the breakers, you may want to start in milder waters. Choosing calm waters may seem to offer an unrealistic expectation that all your adventures will be in a safe, placid setting. Bodies of water such as lakes, shallow slow streams, sounds, and marshes all hold one big advantage, you have the opportunity to practice your paddling techniques and skills in an environment that does not hold additional dangers.

Learning how to paddle, how to steer your boat, how to get in and out of it are going to take practice. Ideally, you want to build your skills in an environment that will allow you to make mistakes, capsize and learn how to handle power boat wake, fatigue, heat exhaustion, and dehydration. You want to enjoy your time on the water as you gain confidence in your kayaking abilities and learn how your boat handles various conditions. You want to know how to react, how your boat responds in small waves and current, a calm body of water with few dangers will be an ideal place to learn how to kayak.

Scout your local area, look for kayak friendly places that don't have swift currents or hazards. Check the internet, research what other paddlers have said about your chosen body of water then go check it out in person. Employees at local sporting good shops or outdoor supply stores will often know the best places to kayak. You are looking for a kayak friendly boat launch, a placid body of water and safe parking nearby. If you find a lake that has fishermen and people with canoes or small sailboats, you have found your place.

In this chapter, you have learned the essentials that you need to get started. Swimming, the ability to paddle, how you are going to transport your boat and a safe place to practice are all a part of getting started. Once you have addressed each of these concerns, you are ready to begin the exciting adventure that is kayaking, you are ready to purchase your boat!

Equipment

The day has arrived, you are finished renting kayaks on vacation or using the complimentary boats at resorts and hotels. You are going to buy your first kayak. As you research kayaks or stand at a big box sporting goods store, you may have already concluded that there is a huge variety of boats. Looking at the boats ranging from a few feet in length to sixteen feet or more can seem daunting. The wide array of colors, the different shapes of the bows and sterns, the width of the cockpits can all be confusing for a beginner.

In this chapter, that confusion will soon be cleared up, and you will be equipped with the knowledge you need to choose a kayak. Along with your kayak, you will also learn how to choose a paddle. Paddles come in a variety of materials and designs and can be as confusing as selecting the right boat. After you have chosen the kayak and the paddle you will learn practical knowledge about transportation and storage of your new purchase.

First, and this is important, not every kayak is ideally suited for every water condition. There are kayaks designed specifically for white water and some designed for the ocean. Boats designed for these specific conditions will be addressed in later chapters. As a beginner, you will need a kayak that is stable and reliable. You need a boat that is suited to fresh water that can also perform admirably well in other non-challenging marine environments such as gentle rivers and salt water with few hazards and small waves.

As tempting as the sleek seventeen-foot ocean kayak may be with its narrow lines, you may want to save that purchase after you have become experienced. You will have more fun in a kayak suited to your experience level and needs as a beginner. Take a few minutes to answer the following questions. The answers you provide will help you as you choose your first kayak.

The kayak you will choose will greatly depend on how you answer the questions below:

- What are you looking for in a kayak?

- Is stability in the water a concern?

- Will you be fishing or taking multi-day trips with your boats?

- Do you prefer the ease of the sit on top kayaks or do you prefer to sit in a cockpit?

- How wide does the cockpit need to be? Wider cockpits are easier to access in or out of the water but boats with narrow cockpits are more stable is challenging conditions.

- How much money have you budgeted for a kayak?

- Did you include money for accessories such as paddle(s), safety equipment and transport?

- Do you intend to carry the kayak on top of your vehicle, on a trailer, or do you prefer an inflatable or fold up model?

- Where will you store the kayak when you are not using it?

Now that you have successfully examined what exactly you want in a boat, you are well on your way to choosing the boat that is right for you. Every kayaker has different needs and concerns, everyone wants to experience a day on the water in his or her own way. By taking the time to address your budget, transportation and even storage, you will be able to focus solely on the boats that fit your criteria, saving you time and taking the confusion out of the process.

Budget is one of the most crucial concerns of any beginner kayaker. Kayaking, like other forms of recreational activity, is accessible to nearly anyone with an interest in the sport. The initial investment can be a few hundred dollars to several thousand depending on your budget and the kayak you choose. As a beginner, you may be apprehensive about spending thousands of dollars on a boat, equipment, and a trailer. This is compounded if you are investing in boats for your family. Fortunately, there are boats available for any budget.

Transportation and storage also pose a conundrum to many beginners. How will the boat be transported? Will it be transported to the water on top of the family minivan or SUV?

Will it be strapped to a kayak trailer? Back home, where will the boat be stored, in the garage or in an outbuilding? Kayaks on average range anywhere from nine to twelve feet in length so storage becomes important, especially if storage space is at a premium in your residence. Consider transportation and storage as you decide which kayak will fit your needs.

Once you have addressed your budget and how you will transport and store the boat, then you can focus on what you want in a boat. What appeals to you about kayaking? Is it a lazy day on a tranquil pond, fishing in a spot no one else knows about, paddling down a river with smooth current? Do you prefer the ease of the sit on top models, or do you prefer the stability of the boats that you sit inside? Is boat's ability to track straight through the water a concern, or do you prefer a roomier wider craft?

No matter what kind of boat you are looking for, a sit on a top model that is light weight or a fishing kayak with storage for bait and tackle, you can find the boat will suit your needs. In the following guide, you will learn about the different kayaks that are designed with the beginner in mind.

Follow the guide below to help you select the perfect kayak for you:

Sit on top kayaks

These boats have flat hulls and are wide which contributes to their stability. They are less likely to tip over or capsize. They are ideally suited for calm waters and perfect for beginner kayakers. They are rigid and often made of strong but heavy plastic. If you are a good swimmer and enjoy spending time in the water or do not mind being exposed to the elements, this style boat is a good choice. Sit on top boats are inexpensive and but there are a few key drawbacks to the design to consider. These boats do not track as straight in the water as other models, they are cumbersome and heavy, and they offer limited storage space for supplies and long journeys. In rivers with more than the gentle current, sit on tops models may easily be tipped over.

Rigid recreational kayaks

These boats have flat or slightly rounded hulls and come in a variety of widths although they tend to be narrower than the sit on top variety. The bows and sterns are pointed and sleeker which adds to the ability of the boat to track straighter in the water. These boats can also maneuver and turn easily and will respond to a novice paddler's steering. Cockpits come in an array of widths from wide open cock pits for ease of accessibility to narrow cockpits offered in more performance oriented models. These boats are ideal for kayaking in a variety of temperatures and conditions. Although not recommended for ocean kayaking, these boats can be used in a wide range of calm to slightly choppy waters and rivers with mild current and small obstacles. Overall, these boats make a more versatile option for beginners as these boats come equipped with storage areas and some models are designed for fishermen. One of the drawbacks of these kayaks is the weight of these boats tend to be heavier than the light weight performance models. They are often constructed of heavy plastic which is durable but not easily repaired. A final detail to consider is these boats do not track as straight or are suitable for rough or challenging conditions as performance or touring kayaks.

Inflatable kayaks

These boats are light weight, can be transported without special equipment and trailers and can be stored inside your home. Constructed from lightweight materials, these boats are often good options when weight, transportation, and storage are all considerations. They also make a good choice for kayakers with limited budgets or are not yet ready to invest in a rigid kayak. Inflatables come in a variety of styles often with flat or slightly rounded hulls for stability and wide cockpits. Depending on the model, they may have spars or additional beams that can be added to improve stability and tracking. Air pumps are required for inflating these boats and many can be fully ready to use in the water in less than twenty minutes. One of the biggest drawbacks of these kayaks is their long-term durability. They are reliable and float due to air pockets but they are not designed to handle the rigors of portaging over rough terrain or constant scrapes and bumps along shallow lake and river bottoms. These boats tend to be sluggish in the water and slow.

Modular kayaks

Available in sit on top as well as rigid recreational styles, these boats combine the durability and stability of recreational models with the ease of transport and storage. They come in pieces that are assembled in only a few minutes and can be transported inside a vehicle and stored in your home. Due to the plastic used in their construction, they handle and respond very close to recreational kayaks and offer similar tracking and reliability. The drawbacks of these models are the same as rigid recreational kayaks and are not designed for challenging conditions. In pieces, they do not weigh very much are but once assembled, they can be heavy.

Folding kayaks

Versatile yet expensive, these boats offer a solution to problems of transportation and storage. These boats come in a variety of hulls and widths from wider recreational models to performance oriented sleeker designs. Their frames offer the reliability and durability of rigid models. They are made of lightweight materials that are easily transported and assembled which makes these boats responsive and fast in the water. Storage for multi-day trips is also similar to rigid kayaks. Although often expensive to purchase, they do not require special equipment to transport or a large amount of space for storage. The drawback to these kayaks is the lower durability as they are often constructed out of lighter weight materials. They also require practice and attention to detail to construct.

Once you have chosen the type of kayak that fits your needs, you will want to consider creature comforts when you are narrowing your search for kayaks. Seat construction and support will be an important consideration for longer journeys in your boat. Adjustable foot pegs are an option to ensure maximum stability and comfort. Padding along the interior rim of the cockpit will make your knees and legs more comfortable. Snaps or other fasteners may be available in addition to padding for the cockpit. This will give you the option for the addition of spray skirt which will keep you warm and dry in rain or cold weather.

After comfort, you will want to consider storage. Storage in a kayak is found in the bow and stern sections. There is also room on the top of the kayak for more items than can be attached with bungee cables. The ability to store items such as dry clothes, safety equipment, food and water, fishing equipment and camping gear may be a key part of your decision to purchase a kayak. When considering storage, also check weight specifications for the kayak you have chosen. Kayaks are designed to safely transport the weight listed. Going over that weight may decrease the stability of the boat in the water and contribute to the boat sitting dangerously low or creating a situation that could lead to the boat capsizing.

After you have successfully chosen the model kayak that is right for you, you will want to find the perfect paddle. Finding the right paddle for you can make the difference between a relaxing day spent on the water or an exhausting ordeal that leaves you feeling drained. If you have researched kayak paddles you have undoubtedly discovered that paddles, like the boats, come in a dizzying array of materials and designs. Fortunately, you are a beginner and you can easily find a paddle that will move you and your boat through the water without a lot of confusion.

Although kayak paddles come in low angle and wide-angle varieties, in metal and plastic and even carbon fiber, to start your kayaking journey you may not need a high angle carbon fiber paddle suitable for rapids. Paddles have their own vocabulary which can be confusing to someone not familiar with kayaking. Although the terms can be confusing, this guide will help to make sense of the chaos. Remember, for your first paddle you want a to choose one that will help you maximize each stroke, reduce fatigue and be easy to use.

Follow this guide to finding the perfect paddle for your boat:

Height and width

Purchase a paddle that fits your height and the width of your cock pit, if your kayak has one. A taller person needs a longer paddle than a shorter person. A person who has a wider cockpit needs a longer paddle than a person of the same height with a narrow cockpit. Charts are readily available at most sporting goods stores and online.

Low angle is a good option

Ideally, a good first paddle will be a low angle paddle designed for slow relaxing strokes. Low angle paddles are designed to minimize fatigue and are suited to hours of slow, steady paddling.

Adjustable is best

Adjustable paddles allow you to determine the angle of the blades. Adjusting the blade angle is important to maintain efficiency and reduce fatigue. Blades that are fixed at different angles from one another will allow you to paddle for longer periods of times with increased efficiency as you move through the water.

Materials

Depending on how many hours or days you intend to paddle, choose a material that fits your needs. Carbon fiber and other state-of-the-art materials are lighter and better choices for long distance journeys. Plastic is durable and less expensive, although heavier than other materials.

The shaft matters

For a beginner, a shaft that is not perfectly round or has a slight bend may help you get the most out of your paddling. Oval shafts that are not perfectly straight will help you reduce fatigue and muscle cramping. Shafts come in widths that are suitable for different size hands so finding the perfect one should be easy. If transportation is a concern, look for paddles that come apart and are easily assembled.

After you have selected the right paddle, there are the important details of transportation and storage that you need to consider. If you have chosen an Inflatable, Modular, or a

Foldable model the transportation and storage of your new kayak will be easy. These kayaks are often small enough to fit in the trunk or back of a vehicle and require minimal space inside your home. Storing these boats in a climate controlled area will lengthen the life of the boat. However, if you have purchased a Sit on top or Rigid Recreational model then you will have to decide how you are going to transport your kayak and store it.

Transportation is going to be a big part of your experience with your new kayak. Carrying your boat to and from your home to your choice of destinations will be almost as important as selecting your boat. How you choose to transport your boat will depend on your vehicle, your physical strength, and your budget. Rigid Recreational kayaks can weigh fifty pounds or more and are cumbersome because of their length to maneuver, details you will want to consider as you examine your options.

Kayak roof mounts and racks are good options if you want an affordable method of transportation. These mounts and holders attach to the factory rack on the top of your vehicle or on the bed of your truck and the roof. Roof mounted systems allow for the easy transport of one or two kayaks. Although affordable the biggest drawback to the roof mounted systems is the physical requirements of loading the boat or boats on to the top of your vehicle. A kayak that weighs over fifty pounds can be difficult to secure snugly into a mount on top of your car by yourself or remove from the mount at your destination. If you do not have reliable assistance, there are also options for fold down mounts and holders available.

If you want to transport multiple boats or have trouble loading the boat onto the roof of a vehicle, you may want to consider the kayak trailer. Kayak trailers attach to the trailer mount located on the back of your vehicle and will require a license plate and insurance depending on your place of residence. They are more expensive than the roof mounted option but are easier to use because of their low height. Another advantage is that you are not limited to two boats as the maximum amount of boats you can carry. Kayak trailers are also popular options if you choose to invest in a longer boat such as the touring or high-performance models favored by ocean kayakers.

Transportation is important but so is storing your kayak. After the purchase of your boat and paddle, you will need a place to store them. Rigid Recreational kayaks are long and can be wide. They are not flexible and require a large amount of space to store properly. A twelve-foot long boat is not going to easily slip into your attic, so you need to have space available.

A garage or outbuilding is an excellent option for these boats, as is a storage facility. Some boats may require climate controlled storage but the heavy plastic boats can be stored in an outbuilding or garage. These may be good options provided the temperature is not prone to great extremes. Storage options include racks that can be purchased or built that hang the kayak on the wall. If your garage is crowded, a good space saving option is storing the boat from a ceiling mounted rack.

You are nearly ready to begin kayaking, but before you put your boat in the water, you will want to purchase the proper safety equipment. In the following chapter, you will learn about safety and how to have a fun, safe time when you take your boat out on the water.

Safety

You have purchased your boat and paddle and are excited to start kayaking, but before you put your boat in the water and start paddling, there are some important pieces of equipment that you need to purchase that may save your life. In addition to equipment, the information in this chapter will help you relax and enjoy kayaking knowing that you have taken steps to avoid dangerous situations and are prepared if you should face a challenge.

Kayaking is a fun, relaxing sport but like any other past time involving a boat and the water, it helps to keep safety in mind. With the right equipment and a common-sense approach, you can have fun with your new kayak in the years to come. With experience comes confidence and being a beginner means that you may need a few pointers about the right equipment to purchase and solid advice. The information in this chapter focuses on safety in calm waters with slow currents. For ocean and white-water kayaking, there are more safety concerns to consider before you begin kayaking in those challenging environments.

After you have made the initial investment of your boat and the major pieces of equipment, there are a few pieces of safety gear that are vital and often required by law. This equipment listed here may save your life or help you assist a kayaker in trouble. While it is unpleasant to think about the worst-case scenarios of boating, it is critical to be prepared and to do what you can to prevent accidents or injury.

Use the following guide as a safety equipment checklist.

Personal Floatation Device

This piece of equipment is critical and should be the first item on your safety checklist. You may be an excellent swimmer but if you should become unconscious, your swimming skills will not help you. These devices look like vests and are clipped or zipped in place around your upper body. The device you choose should be comfortable and designed for kayaking which means that the device will not restrict your ability to paddle or swim. Other devices for power boating or sailing may be designed to blow up when they become wet so be careful to purchase a device designed for kayaking! Many devices come with straps that can be adjusted for a better fit and pockets. Pockets are a bonus as they make good storage for items such as a waterproof camera, a phone in a waterproof case, a whistle and a folding knife. Devices are affordable and should always be worn when you are kayaking.

Whistle

Whistles are required by law and are inexpensive to purchase. They can be found at most sporting goods stores that sell personal floatation devices and should be attached to the device. A whistle is a critical piece of safety equipment because the sound of the whistle travels farther than the sound of the human voice. Also, it takes less effort to blow the whistle then yell and scream for help, a factor that may be important if you capsize and have been floating for hours without food or water.

Folding knife

A small waterproof folding knife located in a pocket of your personal device is an item that you may never need but is critical if you do. In the event of a capsize, a knife may prevent you from drowning if you have become tangled in a line or underwater debris.

Rope or line

A small amount of line or rope measuring ten feet or more is an important piece safety equipment like the knife. You may not need it, but if you do, it becomes critical. If a fellow kayaker becomes incapacitated or injured, attaching the line to his or her kayak will allow you to tow the person to safety. Also, rope can be used to secure your kayak to a dock or boat launch to prevent injury when you are climbing in or out of your kayak. Rope is also essential to safely portage a kayak over many obstacles and may be used to help swimmers that are having difficulty or suffering from an injury.

Waterproof storage box or bag

These boxes and bags are essential for keeping important items such as a spare set of car keys, a first aid kit or food dry. These boxes and bag are often designed to float in the event of a capsize. If you are planning a long journey, water proof storage is essential to preserve food and keep clothes dry especially during the colder months of the year when hypothermia becomes a risk.

Cell phone

Be sure your cell phone is fully charged, you may want to consider a spare power source that you store in the water proof storage on your boat. In an emergency, a cell phone can make a difference, if you become lost or if there is a crisis such as capsize or poisonous snake bite.

First aid kit

Be sure to include a basic first aid kit in your water proof storage. Bandages, antibacterial ointment, and antiseptic wipes are essential. If you are taking medication, be sure to include a days' supply in case of emergency. Be sure to include allergy medication if you are sensitive or allergic to bug bites or stings.

Extra paddle

Most paddles that are designed for kayaking float and can be retrieved if they fall into the water. If your paddle gets away from you, you will have considerable difficulty steering and moving through the water without it. You or someone you are paddling with do not want to be at the mercy of the current.

Portable bilge pump

These small hand-held devices can be stowed on board your boat. They are light, inexpensive and a great piece of insurance to have just in case you damage your boat or your boat springs a leak.

Hat and sunscreen

Sun poisoning and sun burn are just two of the uglier side effects of not preparing for a day on the water, but these two conditions can be minor compared to heat exhaustion or heat stroke. By wearing a hat that has a wide brim that covers your face and neck and using sunscreen you can prevent the dehydration that accompanies sun poisoning and sun burn. Dehydration in conjunction with elevated body temperature can lead to the heat exhaustion or heat stroke. Heat stroke can be deadly if not treated quickly, so wear your hat, use sunscreen and stay hydrated.

More food and water than you need

Staying hydrated especially in warmer temperatures is critical to staying safe on the water. Dehydration can occur at any temperature but is prevalent in heat over ninety degrees or during physical activity. Also, unless you are kayaking in a shade covered creek or river, most large bodies of water offer little to no shade, so hydration is vital. Not only is hydration important to prevent heat related ailments but water and food may become critical. In the unlikely event that you become lost or unable to return to your vehicle due to a fast-moving river current, unforeseen obstacles or a myriad of other challenges, you will need food and water. Your three-hour afternoon kayaking may turn into a six-hour trek if you run into an unforeseen event. A good rule to remember is to always pack more food and water than you need.

The safety equipment listed above may seem a large list of items for an hour or two on the water but the concept of safety gear is to be prepared to any contingency that may arise. Even with diligent monitoring of weather or careful planning of an afternoon on a nearby creek, emergencies can strike at any time. The experienced kayaker knows that being on the water in a small boat far away from help is not where you want to find yourself unprepared.

Once you have assembled your safety equipment, you are ready to go paddling. Just follow these helpful safety tips and you will be able to avoid most causes of accidents and injuries while having a wonderful time in your new kayak.

Safety tips for beginner kayakers:

Do not drink and paddle

This seems like an easy one but it bears repeating. Just because you are in the water doesn't mean the rules no longer apply regarding drinking and operating a vehicle. But it is more than just the law, it is good common sense. Most accidents that lead to serious injury or even death have been attributed to alcohol. You may not have a power boat, but drinking affects your balance, your response time and dehydrates you, therefore it is never a good idea to have a few drinks and kayak. Enjoy your beverages but wait until you safely return to dry land.

Pay attention

You are a kayaker in a boat that is less than fifteen feet long and sits low in the water. Other boaters, particularly power boaters and sail boaters may not see you or may not be able to steer out of your way quickly. It is your responsibility to watch out for them and avoid collisions. Regardless of the laws which state who has the right of way in a powered versus unpowered boat interaction, you must assume that no one can see you and steer accordingly.

Be aware of wildlife

Before you paddle in waters unknown to you, be sure that the river, lake or tidal marsh is safe for boaters. In some areas, large alligators, snapping turtles, water moccasins, rattle snakes, and poisonous varieties of jelly fish make their home in the same environment you wish to kayak. Be aware of any posted warnings and research what animals may be native to the environment. The best way to avoid a confrontation with many dangerous animals is to be knowledgeable about their habits and their habitat.

Stay hydrated

This is critical, don't just rely on water, carry sports drinks that contain salt. Check with your doctor about any medications you may be taking that could make you susceptible to heat related ailments. Before kayaking, be sure to properly hydrate and then continue to stay hydrated while you are boating. If you are paddling with others, be sure they are staying hydrated as well. Learn the signs and symptoms of heat exhaustion and heat stroke and monitor yourself or others for any signs of these ailments.

File a plan

Tell someone where you are going and when you expect to be back. This is especially important if you are kayaking in a body of water you may not be familiar with. Make sure the person can contact emergency personnel with an accurate description of your boats, what you are wearing and where you are. Give coordinates and details such as the boat ramp you are parked at or nearby stores or towns. Details are critical.

Take care when estimating time

Kayaking is not power boating, you are at the whim of the weather, the current and many other unforeseen situations such as downed trees or muscle cramps. If you estimate a short trip down the river will take two hours, plan for three or four. A day trip may become overnight, so be prepared with extra supplies. This is especially true if the body of water you are kayaking is unknown to you.

Accurately assess your capabilities

If you want to kayak for six hours to a destination and you have only kayaked for an hour or two at the most, you may not be ready to make that jump just yet. Kayaking is relaxing and seems to be a sport that will not cause exhaustion or physical exertion but that changes when you begin to kayak for greater periods of time than you are accustomed to. Be honest when you are planning to kayak and you will be less likely to suffer from fatigue and exhaustion related injuries and accidents.

Do not paddle alone

While you are a beginner, it is better to paddle with another person or a group. This may not always fit your schedule but this piece of advice will keep you safe as you gain experience and confidence. There are many kayak tours that are operated by experienced guides that you can join. You may also convince your spouse or friend to take up the sport with you. Once you have gained experience and feel ready to kayak on your own, be sure to file a plan and carry your safety equipment.

Take a safety course

Kayaking, like other forms of boating, has different skills levels from beginner to expert. As a beginner, you may want to take instruction from an expert to prepare you for any challenge. If you would like to learn more about safety and improve your kayaking skills, you may want to consider signing up for a course or weekend kayaking safety clinic.

Cold is just as dangerous as heat

Most beginner kayakers do not venture into their small boats in the dead of winter, but hypothermia is not just a winter phenomenon. The water temperature in spring and fall can drop to dangerously low levels that can cause hypothermia. if you capsize and fall into the water. However, hypothermia is not the only danger. In water that is under sixty degrees, your body can still go into shock which can lead to drowning or cardiac arrest. In water below fifty degrees, hypothermia can result. If you are planning to kayak in these conditions be sure you are wearing the proper safety gear such as a wet suit or other insulated clothing. Hydration, food intake and any sign of even mild hypothermia should be addressed immediately, even if there has not been a capsize.

Be careful of flooded waters

If your favorite river has reached flood stage or the water is higher than normal, it is best to avoid kayaking that day. Flooded rivers and creeks can hide unseen obstacles that can lead to capsize or possess currents capable of moving cars. Rapids and other hazards may also exist that are not normally part of your favorite water trail. It's best to let the water recede back to normal levels.

By following these safety tips, you can be confident that you have taken the necessary steps to prevent accidents, injuries, and most emergencies. These tips are not meant to scare you away from kayaking or present this sport as though it were dangerous, but to help you prepare for any challenge you may meet on the water. Kayaking is fun and relaxing and with the right knowledge about safety, you can enjoy kayaking for years to come.

How to Kayak

Kayaking looks simple, sit in or on top of your kayak, hold on to the paddle and start paddling through the water. Kayaking is simple but there are techniques that you will want to know to get the most out of your time spent on the water. Techniques from the way you hold your paddle to the strokes you use to propel you and your kayak across the water will help you become a better kayaker. By learning and practicing these procedures you can reduce fatigue, prevent accidents and have more fun in your kayak.

Learning how to kayak is easy and the best place to start is out of the water. Before you take the boat off the roof of your car or inflate it at the dock, look for the ideal place to enter the water. Many boat launches and boat ramps are paved and gently slope to the water. There may be a dock with a ladder or a low platform floating in the water. In some locations, you may need to find a dry river bank. Check for rocks and other obstacles if you choose to launch from a river bank or the bank of the marsh.

Once you have chosen the ideal spot to put your boat into the water, it's time to inflate, snap together or remove your kayak from the vehicle and carry it out the water. Launching from a river bank or dock may have its differences but keeping the boat balanced and stable is going to be your priority. When you have secured the boat to the dock or found the ideal place to slide the boat into the water. Use care and move slowly as you enter the boat.

If you are launching from the water or river bank use your paddle to help steady you and the boat. Using your paddle, place it across the back of the boat, just behind the cockpit. One of the blades should be resting on the river bank and the other on the boat. Bend down and grasping the paddle and the cockpit rim for support carefully step into the boat on the side nearest to you. Once you are in the boat, slowly maintaining the boat's balance, sit down in the seat and stretch your legs until your feet reach the foot pegs. Be sure your knees are touching the sides of the kayak at the cockpit and you are seated all the way back. Using your paddle, you are now ready to begin kayaking.

If you are launching from a dock be slow and cautious. You may use a line to tie the kayak to the dock to steady your boat before attempting to enter the kayak. Place your paddle on the dock within easy reach or set it inside the cockpit and slide it into the nose of the boat. Do not step into the kayak as if you were stepping onto the deck of a power boat. Sit on the dock just above the cockpit, holding onto the dock for support slide your feet into the kayak and carefully sit in the boat. Once inside the boat slide your feet into position and adjust your body until your back is supported and the kayak feels stable. If your paddle is on the dock, don't forget to grab it before you untie the line.

With your paddle in your hand, your personal floatation device on and your safety equipment in place, you are in your boat in the water and you are ready. The first step is holding the paddle correctly. Hold the paddle at approximately the width of your shoulders. You may have to adjust the exact positioning to get the most power out your stroke but be careful not to hold your hands too close together as that will require twice the effort to move the blades through the water. When you look down at your hands, they should be relaxed, your fingers firmly around the shaft but not gripping it tightly. A kayak paddle is designed to pull and push the blades through the water and a firm but relaxed grip will help you achieve that motion.

The most common paddle stroke that you will use is the forward stroke. This stroke is your engine, it is the stroke that you will use to power the kayak through the water. It is easy to understand and to master. Holding your paddle, lower the right side blade in the water approximately where your feet rest on their foot pegs. Be careful that you put just the blade in the water. Your right hand will pull the paddle and your left hand closest to the blade in the air pushes at that end. As you are pushing and pulling, your body is slowly, gently rotating in the direction of the blade in the water as you bring it past your body.

The next stroke on the left side is the reverse, once the right blade is past your hips, turn your body and lower the left blade into the water by your feet and raise the right blade out of the water. Pulling the paddle with your left hand and pushing the paddle straight ahead with our right as your body slowly rotates to face the left blade pulling through the water.

Continue alternating the right and left blades in the water. Pay close attention that you are using not only your shoulders, but you core and your back to do the work. The stroke should be gentle and silent, the paddle should not hit the cockpit or side of the boat. Focus on pushing and pulling as you rotate your body until this motion becomes second nature to you. Every motion should be gentle, relaxed and graceful. Mastery of this stroke and the proper technique of pushing, pulling and body rotation will reduce fatigue and allow you to move efficiently and quickly through the water.

You have now practiced going straight but what about turning and steering the boat? At some point, you will want to change direction or need to suddenly alter your course to avoid a hazard. Fortunately, there are two ways to change direction in a kayak.

The first technique is easy and effortless. If you want to turn towards the right drop the right blade into the water just past your right hip, the boat will turn towards the right. The same is true on the opposite side, to turn left, drop the left blade into the water just past your hip. Hold the blade in the water until the kayak has turned the angle you hope to achieve.

The second technique for steering your kayak takes a little more practice to master but will not slow you down like the previous technique. If you want to turn right, drop the left blade into the water as far to the front of the boat as your feel comfortable. Be sure to maintain balance and try not to lean too far forward. Move the blade in a wide arc out from the bow of the boat around in a half circle until you bring as far back to the stern as you can. This technique is known as a sweeping stroke and will steer the boat into a right turn. You may have to complete this stroke more than once to achieve the angle of turn you desire.

Bringing the kayak to a stop or reversing course is simple, the reverse stroke is exactly as it sounds, you will drop one of the blades into the water behind the cockpit and push with the hand closest to the blade and pull with the hand in the air while rotating your upper body as the blade goes in the appropriate direction of the forward stroke. In the simplest terms, you are reversing the forward stroke, completing each movement in reverse. By back-paddling using this stroke, you can bring the kayak to a stop.

You can move your kayak sideways through the water in addition to forward left or right. There are two techniques and both are a little more dangerous as they can create an unstable situation if you are not careful. The first technique is known as the T stroke, you put the blade in the water straight out from the cockpit at a perpendicular angle facing the direction you want to move towards. Carefully, pull the blade through the water towards yourself. Be careful to remove the blade before it gets too close to the boat. This stroke can cause the boat to dip towards the blade and affect the balance of the kayak. If the blade is causing the boat to tip, don't fight it or try to remove the blade from the water, just release it.

A safer although more strenuous technique for moving sideways through the water is the sculling stroke. Place the blade in the water parallel to the boat at arm's length without leaning over. Maintain your balance as you use your upper body to guide the paddle. Move the blade back and forth through the water from the front of the boat to the back over and over. On every return trip of the blade be sure the blade is at an angle to the water. Do not bring the paddle towards you as you continue this stroke, maintain the distance and rotate your body as you change the angle of the paddle. This stroke will move you kayak sideways or parallel.

These strokes are intended to help you steer your boat and propel you forward through the water, but what happens if you run into trouble? Are there any strokes or techniques for emergencies or sudden changes in the water such as power boat wake or other hazardous conditions? In the following paragraphs, you will learn two techniques that can help you reestablish control of your kayak.

One of the simplest and most effective strokes to learn and practice is known as the low brace. This stroke may help you avoid a capsize if your boat begins to tip over. Mastery of this stroke takes practice so you may want to try it a few times in a safe environment before you need it. The low brace allows you to use your paddle to stop the tilting of the boat. When you notice that your boat is dangerously unstable and tilting past your ability to comfortably right it, hold your paddle straight across the cockpit with the blades flat, parallel to the water. Keeping your elbows up as you dip the blade into the water on the side the kayak is tilting towards. The blade should enter the water just behind your hips. With a powerful push of the hand closest to the water and powerful pull from the hand closest to the blade in the air, quickly rotate your body, bringing the opposite hip down as you slightly rotate the blade in the water as you bring it forward in a quick, powerful short stroke.

A similar stroke that is difficult but also effective to avoid capsizing is the high brace. This stroke will require practice to master, preferably in a quiet body of water that is safe, and not when you are alone. To perform the high brace, hold the paddle straight across the cockpit with your elbows down. The paddle should be roughly the height of your shoulders. The blade will be parallel to the water with the curved side facing down. Put the blade in the water on the side that is tilting and quickly rotate it back toward you as you rotate your body. Use the hand on the opposite end of the shaft top to help turn the paddle while keeping the opposite side as close to the cockpit as you can. This will stop the kayak from tipping over, you can use your hips to bring the boat back to an upright position. Like the low brace, this stroke is short, quick and powerful.

When you have decided to return to dry land, you will want to paddle to the river bank, dock or boat launch. By learning how to safely climb into your kayak on land, in the water or on a dock, you have also discovered how to exit the kayak as well. The same rules and techniques apply. Use your paddle to steady yourself and brace the kayak on a river bank, tie up to dock if you can, stay low as you exit the kayak at a dock. Being careful to maintain the balance of the boat at all times.

As you gain more experience, you will discover that there are dozens of strokes that are variations of these fundamental techniques that are listed in this chapter. Some of the strokes that you will learn as you master the sport of kayaking are difficult for beginners and may be hazardous to attempt until you gain experience in the water. As you kayak, you will become more proficient at moving your kayak, steering it and avoiding capsize. Once you have mastered the basic strokes, you will be ready to try variations and the infamous rolls. If you decide to give ocean or white water kayaking a try, you will also learn new techniques that will be an addition to the foundation that you have already established by your commitment to practicing and mastering the strokes in this chapter.

Ocean and White Water

In the previous chapter, you learned what equipment to purchase and how to paddle in fresh water conditions. Fresh water conditions are calm, placid lakes and slow-moving rivers but may include salt water marshes. The reason that you learned about this type of kayaking is due to safety, beginners find the ocean and white water far more challenging and hazardous.

As you gain experience kayaking, you may be tempted to try the other variations of the sport. In this chapter, you will discover a brief introduction to the ocean and white water. You may find a new way to enjoy kayaking and begin planning your next trip with the salt water waves or class 2 rapids in mind.

At the beginning of this book, the origins of kayaking were discussed and you may have been surprised to learn of its oceanic heritage. Kayaking began on the sea, as a mode of transportation and for acquiring food. The indigenous people of North America used their boats to move from Alaska and Canada to Greenland, making the dangerous crossing of the

North Atlantic in boats made of seal skin and whale bone. In our modern times, the boats used for ocean, also referred to as open water kayaks may be made of different materials but the design is similar and the dangers are the same.

Ocean kayaking is characterized first and foremost by the distinct type of kayak used for navigating through waves and tides, boats that can steer through the wind and rough seas. Although some Rigid recreational kayaks can be used on calm sea water, these are not true ocean kayaks. The kayaks used in heavy waves are very long, with narrow bows and sterns ending in points that sometimes are designed to tip upward. The hulls are v shaped and the cockpits are narrow, requiring a spray skirt. Ocean kayaks may also have additional steering mechanisms such as rudders and skegs. These kayaks are often referred to as touring kayaks and are ideally suited for multi-day journeys across rough and calm waters. The investment in a good quality touring kayak can be thousands of dollars and due to their length, a kayak trailer may be a requirement.

Ocean kayaking is physically and mentally demanding, the risks are greater, the potential dangers are daunting and you must pay attention to conditions with a focus not required on a calm lake. Ocean water is often colder and requires the use of insulated clothing. Being a strong swimmer is a must and being physically able to right your boat when rolled over is an essential skill. Yet, this type of kayaking is true to the roots of the sport and there is a feeling of accomplishment that comes with mastering the challenge of ocean kayaking.

On the opposite end of the spectrum and time is white water kayaking. A thoroughly modern invention, this type of kayaking has its roots in the Victorian age. When the Europeans discovered kayaking, the first bodies of water they attempted to traverse were rivers in the gorges of Europe. Rapids, rocks, waterfalls and other hazards did not deter these intrepid kayakers. Over a century later, white water kayaking has developed a following and is represented in the Summer Olympics.

White water kayaking is the domain of thrill seekers, adrenaline junkies and the young at heart. It evokes images of kayakers diving off rocks into the waters below, class four rapids and hazards waiting for them as they slip around rocks and obstacles, being enveloped by angry white water. This is an accurate description of the sport but does not represent the entire picture. White water kayaking is also class 1 rivers that move with a current that propels you down the river and past few obstacles. Yet, even though this type of kayaking can be relaxing, it requires physical strength, excellent swimming skills, specialized equipment and usually a helmet.

The kayaks designed for white water are prized for their agility and the ability to respond in a Nano-second yet they appear strange and short. These boats are often much shorter than other kayaks averaging seven feet or less in length, the bows and sterns are rounded or come to blunt ends. These boats are light, fast and can turn with the slightest effort. These kayaks are specialized equipment and they are affordable starting at a thousand dollars. While they are not suited for other types of kayaking other than white water, they can be used in calm waters but with less efficiency and increased difficulty to steer and track.

White water kayaking requires a skill set and strokes that must be executed with precision and power, unlike other types of kayaking. White water kayaking can be an exciting past time but you may want to consider seeking professional guidance before you jump right in. investing in a class from instructors who specialize in this hazardous but thrilling variation of the sport is suggested if you want to learn how to navigate white water safely. Once you are proficient and have all your new safety gear and equipment, you can enjoy the thrill of racing down a river gorge at a high rate of speed.

Destination Kayaking and Multi-Day Adventures

Your kayaking journey has led you to this chapter, a destination that may have taken you months or years to reach. As you journeyed from beginner to expert kayaker, you also started branching out from day trips to an interest in longer adventures. You may have found yourself planning a vacation to a destination that would be ideal for kayaking.

Destination kayaking and multi-day adventures require an understanding of basic strokes such as those found in this book, they require endurance and some degree of physical stamina. Even the most relaxing guided tours require a few hours of paddling every day. If you have practiced your strokes, spent time on the water honing your skills and gaining experience, you are ready for a vacation of kayaking and touring.

Depending on your budget, you may want to consider investing in a touring kayak if you decide that kayaking for several days at a time is a part of your future. Touring kayaks are longer, track straight, have more storage capacity and are often lighter than other recreational kayaks. To begin your multi-day kayaking adventures, the kayak that you purchased as a beginner will be fine in calm waters and slow-moving bodies of water.

Destination kayaking is one of the greatest pleasures of owning a kayak. There is something thrilling about selecting a destination based solely on the reviews on a kayaking web site or an article in a kayaking magazine. Finding a spot on the map that is known for its pristine waters and access to rivers, bays, and lakes can be exciting.

Planning a vacation that includes your kayaks can be a joy if you follow a few simple tips:

Security

If you are staying at a hotel or vacation rental, be sure security is available or you have a safe place to store your kayaks when not in use. Kayaks can be expensive and you don't want anything to happen to your investment.

Location is critical

If you plan to spend all your time exploring the destination, be sure you find a vacation home that is on the water or close to your chosen body of water. Having your own private dock on a lake or river can make a kayaking vacation even more fun.

Don't forget to file a plan

Even though you are miles from home, let someone know where you are going and what time you will be back.

Use additional lines

If you are traveling on the interstate, be sure your boats are strapped securely to the roof of your vehicle or kayak trailer, use additional lines if necessary. Also, be prepared that having kayaks on your roof may alter your gas mileage and make noise as the wind passes over and around them as higher rates of speed.

Another wonderful way to spend a vacation on the water is the multi-day adventure. You can plan one of these trips yourself by researching water and paddling trails. These vacations combine camping and kayaking, a mixture of relaxing by the camp fire at night and paddling during the day. If you plan a multi-day adventure be sure to include water proof bags for your clothes and camping supplies. You will also want to carry more food and water than you need and have a supply of medicine. Don't forget to file a plan before setting out.

A variation of the multi-day adventure that you plan yourself is the guided kayaking tour. These tours, also called eco-tours, are ideal for kayakers with fundamental skills. They are often led by experienced kayakers, are safe and are excellent opportunities to experience places and nature that you may never have seen otherwise. You will be kayaking in a group with other like-minded people that enjoy your past time. The camaraderie and thrill of visiting new places by water is a big draw of these adventures.

Guided tours can also include naturalists and other experts in wildlife native to a region which can add to your enjoyment of the experience. These tours often have themes such as bird watching, dolphin or whale watching or exploration of a state park or sanctuary. Tours to fishing villages and coastal lighthouses can also be enjoyed in a multi-day guided kayaking adventure. The cost for these tours is often quite affordable and will give you a chance to test your skills and stamina by paddling for several days under the guidance of more experienced kayakers. By the end of a guided tour, you will be proficient at paddling and learn a few things about life on the water along the way.

Choosing to vacation or spend several days on a guided kayaking tour can be a wonderful way to enjoy the sport of kayaking. If you have the desire to experience kayaking for more than a few hours, see nature in a new way and enjoy a slower pace, then a kayaking vacation or adventure may be right for you. Load your kayak and your gear, the water is waiting.

Conclusion

You have made an exciting journey. You started as someone interested in kayaking. You may have rented a boat on vacation but did not own a kayak of your own. Your interest in this sport was piqued by an experience or maybe watching a group of kayakers enjoying their favorite past time on a lake or at the beach. At some point, you made the decision to purchase a boat and learn how to paddle.

In this book, your journey began as you discovered the history of kayaking and how it left the freezing cold of the North to become at home thousands of years later on summer lakes and autumn rivers. Kayaking has adapted to modern times, never staying stagnant. Its legions of loyal devotees have grown, shaping the sport as they have changed what they wanted out of kayaking. Kayaking means fishing, ecotours, paddling adventures, day trips, white water adventure and ocean paddling in the modern century and all of those are right, kayaking has grown, adapted and yet remains true to its roots.

You navigated the complex terrain of sporting goods stores and chose your kayak from the vast array of styles and materials. You picked out your paddle and purchased safety equipment.

You learned about boating safety and discovered that being prepared for an emergency makes a day on the water much more enjoyable.

In the chapters of this book, you practiced your paddling techniques, learned strokes for steering and how to move your boat through the water efficiently and safely. You also learned how to avoid a capsize and the techniques for climbing in and out of your boat to eliminate the anxiety of ending up in the water!

As you made the journey from beginner to experienced kayaker you may have shown an interest in the other types of kayaking, the adrenaline fueled white water variety and the physically demanding ocean or open water paddling as it is often called. Finding out that you may need new equipment and more safety equipment may have been a surprise but you decided that you may give the other types of kayaking a try one day.

Finally, you journeyed to the vacation planning part of kayaking, when kayaking has become a part of who you are. You enjoy your time on the water and are always looking for new places to explore. Your kayak is racking up miles because you are taking it with you wherever you go. Your interest in multi-day trips and guided kayaking tours is where you find yourself on this journey, ready to begin the next adventure in your kayak.

As you continue to gain experience and grow in your confidence and abilities, enjoy every moment you spend in the water whether it is a quiet lake or a swiftly moving river. The time that you spend kayaking is time that is not wasted, it will be your refuge and your way of getting away from it all. No matter where your kayaking journey takes you, take a moment to reflect how far you have come with the paddle in your hands and the boat under you, gliding through the water, the stress of the world left behind in the wake of your kayak.

Win a free

kindle
OASIS

Let us know what you thought of this book to enter the sweepstake at:

http://booksfor.review/kayak

Printed in Great Britain
by Amazon